a coloring boo
Ancient India

Many of the pictures inside are from ancient stone carvings, which were originally painted with beautiful colors. Through the centuries the paint has disappeared, but if you color the drawings brightly, you will see how these glorious monuments once might have looked.

The Man From Harappa

The ancient civilization of the Indus Valley was first discovered in modern times at the city of Harappa. This had been a thriving place, contemporary with the Mesopotamian civilizations with which the Harappan peoples traded. This figure appears similar to some found in Mesopotamia, and might even be from there. The ancient Indus cities had straight streets and bathrooms in houses.

From a statuette from Mohenjo-Daro, 3rd millennium B.C. National Museum, Karachi

Drawings by Nancy Conkle

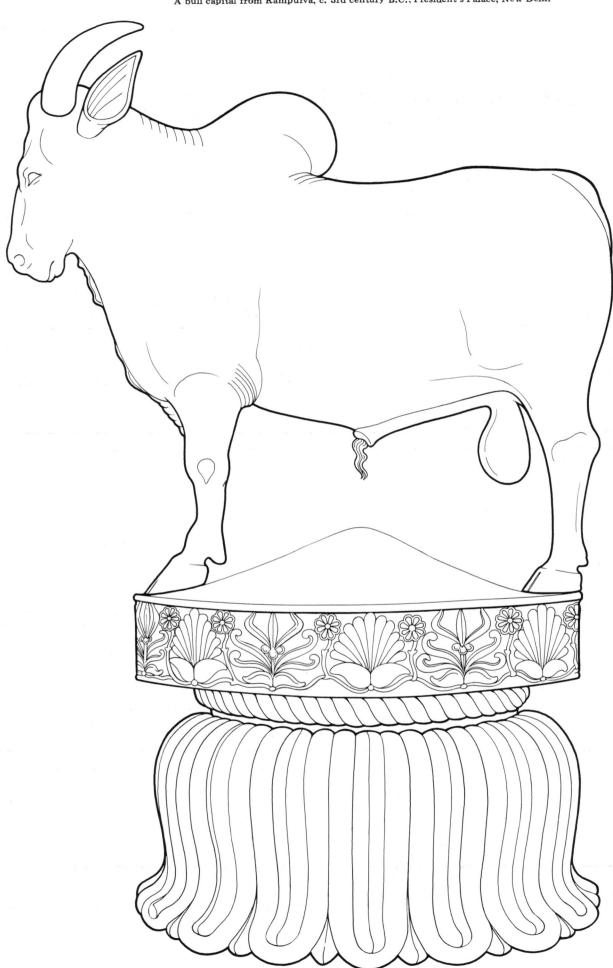

A lion capital from Sarnath, 3rd
century B.C.; Sarnath Museum

While the bull, opposite,
was an Indian motif, the
lion, a royal symbol, was
imported from western
Asia. A great wheel, a solar
symbol, once stood atop
these lions at the top of a
capital which capped a tall
Asoka pillar. The lion was
also a symbol of the family
of Sakyamuni Buddha,
who is often shown with
lions and called a lion.

Alexander the Great de-
feated Darius III in 330
B.C., and then took over
Darius's eastern provinces.
With the fall of the Ach-
aemenian empire, unem-
ployed craftsmen found
new patrons at the Maurya
court in India. About the
time of King Asoka, 272-
231 B.C., tall stone pillars
were erected, topped by
great capitals like this one
from Sarnath.   The pil-
lars represented the World
Axis, separating heaven
and earth. The palmettes
and rosettes are like those
found on Achaemenian
stone work, which used an
adaptation of Greek mo-
tifs.

The Bo Tree by the River Nairanjana where the Buddha found enlightenment; here he remained, not stirring for seven days, in his cross-legged position, experiencing bliss. "Never will I stir from here until I have attained absolute wisdom," he said. Here worshippers are at the path the Buddha took after his illumination.

From the south pillar, Sanchi, 1st century B.C.

Yakshi the Tree Nymph

Sanchi was a very important early Buddhist monastery. *Stupas*, mounds of earth with relics or a sacred tree, were built there; they were enclosed by railings around which worshippers walked. At Sanchi there were wonderfully beautiful stone carvings such as this *yakshi*. *Yakshis* were female spirits of the forest, associated with fertility and abundance.

From the eastern gate, Sanchi, 1st century B.C.

From Sanchi, 1st century B.C.

Skanda, the son of Siva, became the lord of war. He rode on a peacock, the killer of serpents, called
Paravani, which meant the year. The peacock is the killer of Time and a symbol of immortality.
At Sanchi the peacock may have represented the Buddha Amitabha-Amitayus, immortality.

From a relief from Amaravati, 2nd century A.D.

Ancient Animals

Genii riding on goats, from reliefs at Sanchi, 1st century B.C.

From Bharhut Stupa, 1st century B.C.; Indian Museum, Calcutta

Queen Maya's Dream

On a midsummer's night at the grove of Lumbini, Queen Maya (Maya means illusion) dreamed that a splendid white elephant walked three times around her couch, trumpeting triumphantly, and struck her on the right side. When the queen awoke, she asked what this meant. The Brahmans said that it meant she would soon have a boy, who would become a king of the universe if he stayed at home or a Buddha if he abandoned the world.

From Bharhut Stupa, 1st century B.C.; Indian Museum, Calcutta

The Deer Park

The Bodhisattva or future Buddha appears as a golden deer, having rescued a drowning man (bottom scene). The ungrateful man tells the king where the deer is to be hunted; the deer tells the king how ignoble the man is; the king venerates the deer.

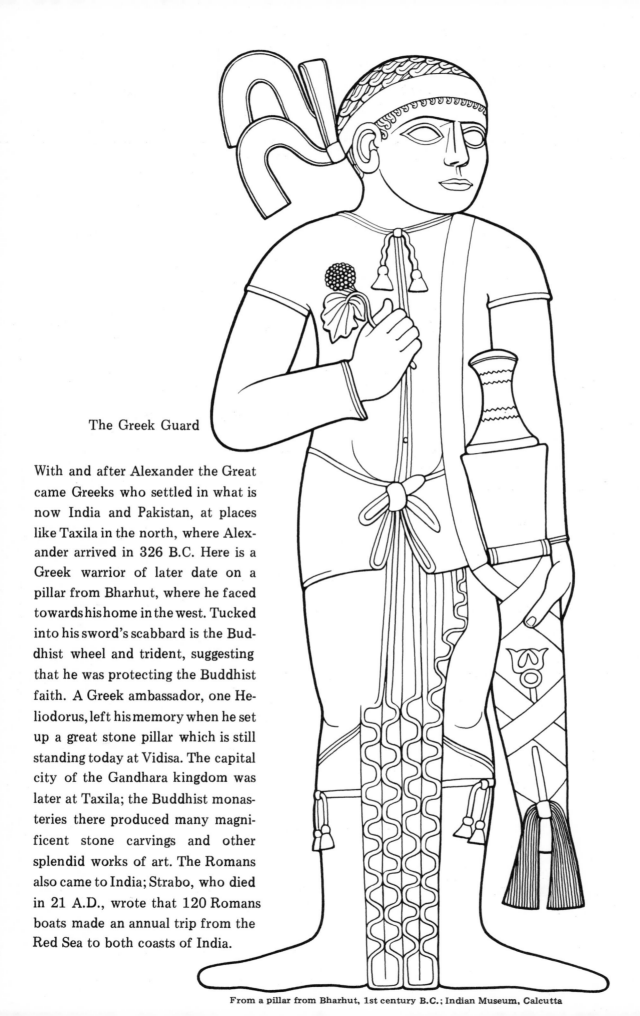

The Greek Guard

With and after Alexander the Great came Greeks who settled in what is now India and Pakistan, at places like Taxila in the north, where Alexander arrived in 326 B.C. Here is a Greek warrior of later date on a pillar from Bharhut, where he faced towards his home in the west. Tucked into his sword's scabbard is the Buddhist wheel and trident, suggesting that he was protecting the Buddhist faith. A Greek ambassador, one Heliodorus, left his memory when he set up a great stone pillar which is still standing today at Vidisa. The capital city of the Gandhara kingdom was later at Taxila; the Buddhist monasteries there produced many magnificent stone carvings and other splendid works of art. The Romans also came to India; Strabo, who died in 21 A.D., wrote that 120 Romans boats made an annual trip from the Red Sea to both coasts of India.

From a pillar from Bharhut, 1st century B.C.; Indian Museum, Calcutta

The *stupa* gate at Bharhut had stone pillars carved with gorgeous figures like these. On the left is Chlakoka Devata, a tree nymph who represents the life force, on an elephant which represents the life-giving force of the waters. On the right, is Sudarsana Yakshi, or the Yakshi beautiful to look at, on a *makara*, a water monster.

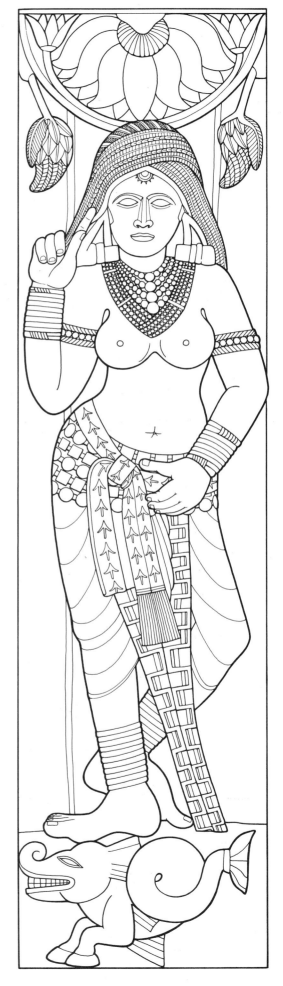

Pillars from Bharhut, 1st century
B.C. ; Indian Museum, Calcutta

Makaras

A *makara* was a crocodile-like mythological monster of the
deep symbolizing good luck and the life-force of the waters.
This one was on a *stupa* railing at Bharhut and the *makara*
opposite was on a beam-end on a *torana* or gateway there.

From Bharhut, 1st century B.C.; Indian Museum, Calcutta

From a beam end on a gate from Bharhut, 1st century B.C.; Indian Museum, Calcutta

The horseman opposite seems to have led a royal procession to Bharhut *stupa*, where he was shown on the eastern gateway *(torana)*. He carries the royal insignia. It is topped by a birdman *(kinnara)* similar to what may once have been on top of Heliodorus's pillar at Vidisa, as this sculpture was dedicated by a gentleman from that very town.

Roundels of open lotus blossoms often appear at Bharhut and at later sites. The lotus symbolized transcendence; this man must be in a transcendent state.

From a railing from Bharhut, 1st century B.C.; Indian Museum, Calcutta

From a pillar from Bharhut, 1st century B.C.; Indian Museum, Calcutta

The Standard Bearer

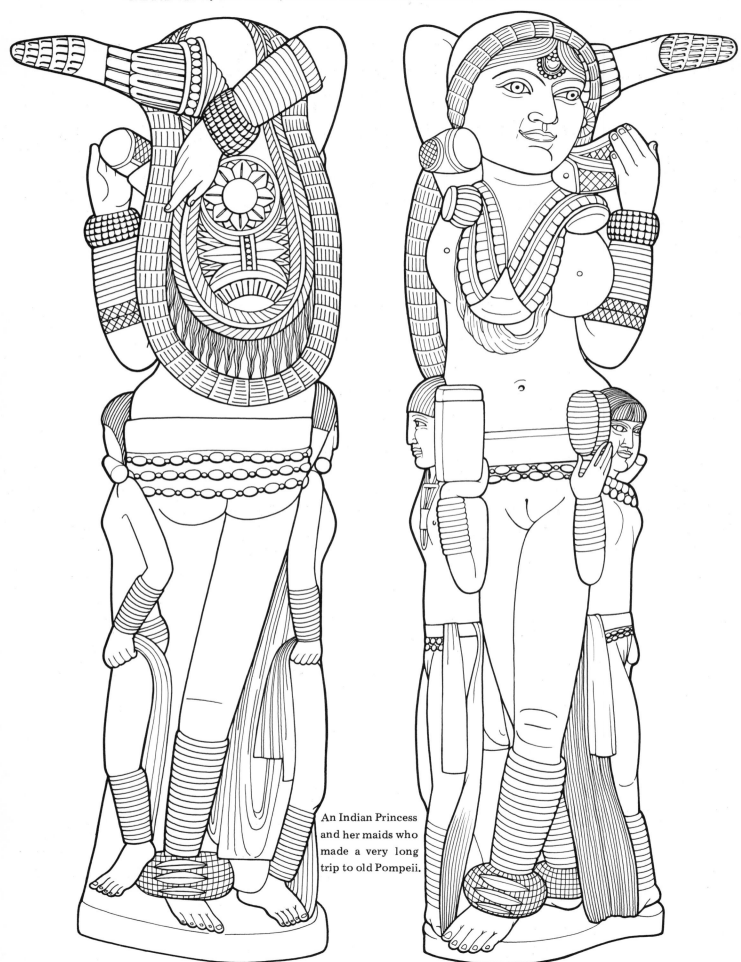

An Indian Princess
and her maids who
made a very long
trip to old Pompeii.

A Bodhisattva

Maitreya was the personification of love. A bodhisattva was a future Buddha, a very perfect being who had attained enlightenment, or *bodhi*, but was willing to help others do so before he himself entered nirvana.

From Takht-i-Bahi, Pakistan, 2nd century A.D.; Lahore Museum

A terracotta group from Ahicchattra, Gupta, 5th century A.D.; National Museum, New Delhi

Ganga the River Goddess

Ganga personifies the Ganges River; here she stands on her *makara*. Ganga was beloved by Siva, and this figure was originally at the entrance to the Siva temple at Ahicchattra. Long, long ago the world had no water. Then a holy man, Bhagiratha, so impressed Ganga that she agreed to come down to the earth. And soon thereafter a great river appeared in Siva's hair. Now there was water.

Urvasi as a Centauress

Nara and Narayana brought the message of love to the world. They were the sons of Righteousness (Dharma) and Nonviolence (Ahimsa), his wife. One day Narayama hit his thigh, and a beautiful nymph, an *apsaras*, Urvasi, appeared from it. An *apsaras* can change her form, and she can also cause madness. Urvasi's son was Vasistha, the wealthy, a lord of progeny, an ancestor of the human race. Another of her sons was Agasti, the Mountain Mover, who represented the power of teaching. He taught grammar, medicine and science.

PREACHING BUDDHA from Sarnath, c. 475 A.D.; Sarnath Museum

The Sarnath Buddha, left

Sakyamuni Buddha is preaching the Four Noble Truths, which were suffering, the cause of suffering, removing the cause (the cure), and the way which leads to removing the cause. One should avoid the extremes of self-indulgence and self-mortification and take the Middle Path. That meant having right views, right thoughts, right action, right speech, right work, right effort, right mindfulness and right meditation.

Another Magnificent Buddha

This magnificent sculpture was the gift of Yasadina the monk, and is inscribed in Gupta letters ". . . let it be for attaining supreme knowledge by his parents, teachers and all living beings."

From Cave I, Ajanta, 6th century A.D.

Ajanta Cave Paintings

One day in the last century, some British soldiers in western India were told by a cowherd of some "tiger lairs." The caves at Ajanta were thus discovered; they were full of the most magnificent wall paintings, ceiling paintings and sculpture imaginable, dating from the 5th century A.D. onward. On the opposite page is the Bodhisattva Padmapani, the Lotus (padma) Bearer. He wears a crown with blue sapphires as a crown prince of Buddhahood. He performs the duty of Buddha until Maitreya returns to this world. On this page is a version of Queen Maya, the soon-to-be mother of Sakyamuni Buddha. She has just told King Suddhodana, her husband and soon to be the Buddha's father, about her great dream (see earlier in this book), and here she is shown waiting for an interpretation of the dream. Queen Maya sometimes appears like a yakshi, or tree nymph.

The King of Mithila (next page)

Prince Mahajanaka (formerly Sakyamuni), having a bath of sixteen pitchers of perfumed water, is shown making his resolve to renounce this world. Before this scene, Mahajanaka, while sailing with his merchandise for Suvannabhumi, was shipwrecked—and saved by the goddess Manimekhala, who returned him to Mithila. There he married Savila, the daughter of the king (that very king had earlier killed Mahajanaka's father, Aritthajanaka.) But by the marriage Mahajanaka soon became king himself. Then he renounced everything, for pomp and luxury did not appeal to the Bodhisattva. The dancers on our back cover tried in vain to turn him from his resolve.

The King of Mithila

The Princess Irandati on a Swing

The princess, trying to find a husband, gathered all the flowers of the Himalaya and made a bed of them, and then she danced and sang a sweet song and, apparently, went swinging.

The White Elephant

The elephant was the royal animal on which the king rode and was used mightily in war. A white elephant is an earthly cloud, which attracts real clouds and is valuable for making rain. White elephants are still valued more than all others. Airvata was the white elephant on which Indra, the king of the gods, rode. Airvata's queen was Abhramu, the Cloud Binder.

From Cave I, Ajanta, 6th century A.D.

Ganesa, the Lord of All Categories, right

Gana means a category, or a collection, of things. Ganesa is the patron of schools and of letters. He is the god of learning. He rules over the assembly of the gods. He is worshipped at the start of every enterprise. The elephant head represents the large being united to the small, man. Siva was his father and Parvati was his mother.

From Samalaji Maitraka, 5th century A.D.; Barooa Museum

Brahma, the Immense Being

He is the Indestructable, The Creator of the World, the Supreme Ruler, the Source of all Knowledge. Brahma has four heads; he once had five, but one was lost by the fire from Siva's third eye. He is colored red. He rides on a swan or goose, which symbolizes knowledge. In his four hands he holds a sceptre, a ladle, beads, a bow, a jug.

From Aihole, 6th century A.D.; Prince of Wales Museum of Western India, Bombay

A Ram,
the pet of Agni, Fire

Agni was the eldest son of Brahma.
Agni, like fire, was colored red, too.

Vishnu the Pervader of All Existence, on Sesha, the Remainder of destroyed universes, king of Serpents, also called Ananta the Endless

"In my four hands are a conch (representing the origin of existence), a wheel (the mind), a mace (the power of knowledge) and a lotus (the universe). The four arms represent the four aims of life: pleasure, success, righteousness and liberation." When Vishnu descends to the world, he comes as an avatar or incarnation, like Nrshima. Vishnu is always black or dark blue, with a yellow veil on his hips.

From Cave III, Badami, Western Chalukya; c. 578 A.D.

The Naga Raja and his Queen

Nagas were half serpent, half human, courageous and violent, and lived in the underworld in beautiful palaces. Sesha, opposite, was one of the three naga kings. A naga was also a super human being.

From Cave 19, Ajanta, c. 500 A.D.

Varaha, or Vishnu as the Cosmic Boar, rescuing the goddess Earth

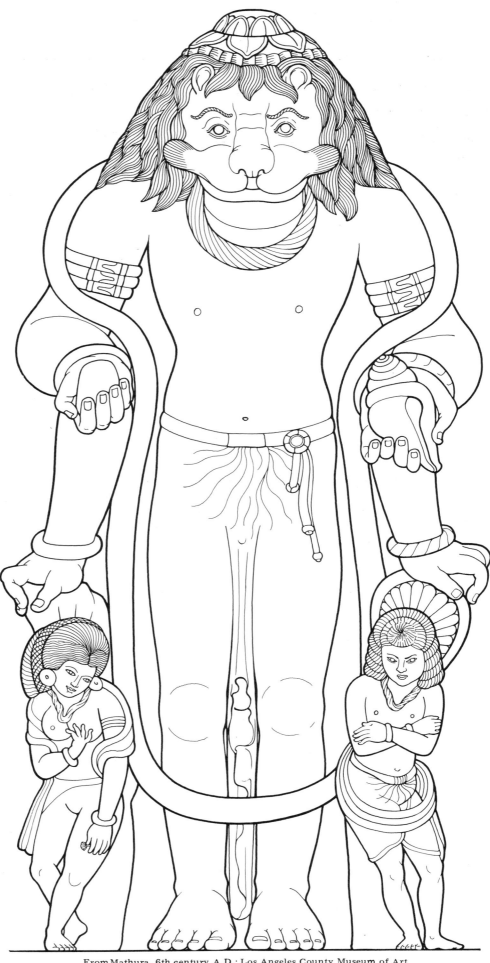

Nrsimha

Hiranyakasipu (Golden
Vesture) had a pious son,
Prahlada, who worshipped
Vishnu. But this father
cruelly punished his good
boy, and finally decided to
kill him. Hiranyakasipu
could not himself be killed
either during the daytime
or at nighttime, or indoors
or outdoors, or by man or
by beast. So Vishnu came
at twilight (not day or
night) as a lion-headed man
(not man nor beast) and in
a porch pillar (not inside or
out). He then slew bad Hiranyakasipu.

From Mathura, 6th century A.D.; Los Angeles County Museum of Art

Flying Vidyadharas

—or Bearers of Wisdom. These are helpful aerial spirits having magic powers. They live in the northern mountains. Sometimes they marry humans, who then become Vidyadharas, too.

From the Mahisasuramardini cave, Mamallapuram, 7th century A.D.

Durga (prior page)

There was once a long war between the gods and the antigods, who were led by Mahisa (the Powerful). Mahisa won the war, and the gods wandered all about the earth. Then Siva and Vishnu caused a blazing ball of fire to come from the mountain of the gods, and this became the goddess Durga (Beyond Reach). She rode out on a red lion and defeated the antigods and Mihisa, who, as a buffalo, was the symbol of death. And then Durga restored heaven to the gods.

A Famous Vrksaka

—or tree goddess, again, representing the life force and fertility. Her missing arms and legs were probably entwined in the boughs of a tree.

The Sungod Surya

right

The Sun is on a lotus (not shown) in his chariot, which has only one wheel and is driven by seven golden horses. Aruna, the Red One, the deity of dawn, drives the chariot and shades the world from the Sun's brightness.

From Gyaraspur, c. 800 A.D.; Central Archaeological Museum, Gwalior

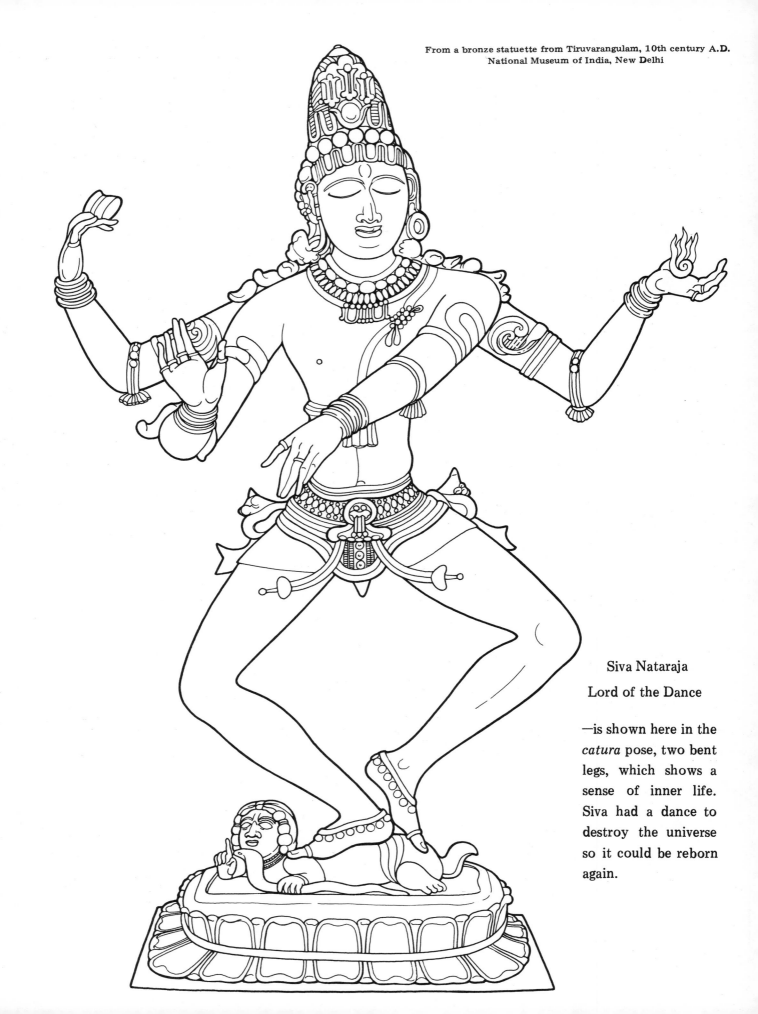

From a bronze statuette from Tiruvarangulam, 10th century A.D.
National Museum of India, New Delhi

Siva Nataraja

Lord of the Dance

—is shown here in the *catura* pose, two bent legs, which shows a sense of inner life. Siva had a dance to destroy the universe so it could be reborn again.

From a South Indian bronze statuette, 15th century A.D.

Parvati

—Daughter of the Mountain, wife of Siva and reincarnation of Sati, Siva's first wife. Parvati is the mother of Ganesa and is the chief of all the elves and spirits who wander about the earth.

From a bronze statuette from Tamil Nadu, 10th century
A.D.; National Museum of India, New Delhi

Krishna and Kaliya

Kaliya (from *kala*, time)
had contaminated the
waters at Vrindavana,
and Krishna, as an in-
carnation of Vishnu,
made the serpent re-
pent by dancing on him.
Thus Krishna conquers
time.

Sakti (Energy)

Sakti was Siva's first wife, and rode on a tiger which represented the power of Nature. Is this tiger part elephant ? ?

From the Temple of Muktesvara, Bhuvanesvara, 10th century A.D.

Siva Nataraja

Here he is doing the *andanda tandavaa*, the dance of bliss on top of Apasmara, who symbolizes ignorance, whom Siva had just vanquished at Chidamba-ram, the center of the universe, that is, within the Heart. He danced to "release the Countless Souls of men from the snare of illusion." The fire represents destruction.

Rahu, the Antigod, lost his head
because of the Moon. However,
his head stayed alive and tried to
eat the moon, colored white.

From the Temple of the Sun, Konarak, 13th century A.D.

From Bundelkhand, northeastern Central India, 11th century A.D.; State Museum, Lucknow

The Bodhisattva Avalokitesvara, left, making the lion roar, that is, preaching the doctrine of enlightenment. He is also known as Padmapani, "Lotus-in-Hand," whom we have seen before. He has a trident, Siva's weapon, and unending compassion and a sublime indifference. He sits in "kingly ease." This page has a splendid danseuse.

A bronze figure from Western Chalukya, 12th century A.D.; National Museum of India, New Delhi

"I'm writing for my free, gorgeous Bellerophon catalog."